Doing Business in the U.S.

BDO

Doing Business in the U.S.

BDO
Binder Dijker Otte

The aim of this booklet, which has been prepared for the exclusive use of BDO and its clients, is to provide the background information needed for setting up and running a business in the U.S.

It is written in general terms and is not intended to be comprehensive. Advice should be sought from the BDO office with which you normally deal.

BDO is a leading international accounting organization offering clients professional auditing, accounting, tax, financial and management advisory services, nationally and internationally.

From its beginning in 1963 as an affiliation of prominent national firms in North America and Europe, BDO is now an international firm with 385 offices in 57 countries with over 14,300 partners and staff.

Well established as an international organization with common operating standards and systems worldwide, BDO also benefits from the calibre of its highly regarded constituent national member firms. For every international engagement, BDO draws upon a combination of specialized and local strengths uniting professionals to deliver national and international expertise as and when and where needed.

BDO's policy is established and its execution is supervised by an Executive Committee of senior partners from eight member firms supported by an International Secretariat. Each committee member is responsible for BDO's operations in a specified geographic area of the world. The Executive Committee is aided by specialist committees for training, development of services and for quality control. Meetings of International Liaison Partners, one partner from each member firm, ensure that BDO's development takes full account of each country's perspective.

© 1988 Binder Dijker Otte

First Edition 1988

ISBN 0 946295 61 1

Printed by Marshment and White
Bradford on Avon Wiltshire

Contents

Preface

Who should read this booklet?

This booklet should be read by anyone who is thinking of establishing a business in the U.S. either as a separate entity, as a subsidiary of an existing overseas company, or anyone who is considering coming to work or living permanently in the U.S.

Scope

Doing Business in the U.S. describes the business environment and the financial and legal implications of running, or working for, the U.S. branch of a company based outside the U.S. All the important issues are included, but it is nearly impossible to discuss every subject in detail within this format. If you would like more information, Seidman & Seidman, the U.S. firm of BDO, publishes a wide range of booklets which examine the issues raised here in greater depth.

Part One

The Business Environment

1. General information

The U.S. is one of the world's largest and most vigorous business markets. Its population currently numbers 236 million; by the year 2000 it is expected to surpass 267 million (See Exhibit 1). The country's gross national product (GNP) is now $3,663 billion and continues to rise, with current per capita annual disposable income averaging $10,887. The unit of currency is the dollar, divided into 100 cents.

The U.S. economy is growing at a rate of 2 to 3% annually. Its expansion is based on an active and growing demand for new and better products and services.

Exhibit 1   **POPULATION DISTRIBUTION**

	1970	1980	1984	1990	2000
Northeast:					
New England	11.8	12.3	12.6	12.7	12.8
Mid-Atlantic	37.2	36.8	37.2	35.7	33.6
Total Northeast	49.0	49.1	49.8	48.4	46.4
Midwest:					
East North Central	40.3	41.7	41.6	42.4	41.6
West North Central	16.3	17.2	17.5	17.9	18.1
Total Midwest	56.6	58.9	59.1	60.3	59.7
South:					
South Atlantic	30.7	37.0	39.5	43.1	49.0
East South Central	12.8	14.7	15.0	16.1	17.2
West South Central	19.3	23.7	26.1	28.3	32.7
Total South	62.8	75.4	80.6	87.5	98.9
West:					
Mountain	8.3	11.4	12.6	15.4	20.1
Pacific	26.5	31.8	34.2	37.5	42.4
Total West	34.8	43.2	46.8	52.9	62.5
Total	203.2	226.6	236.3	249.1	267.5

Source: U.S. Department of Commerce

Geography

The U.S. is a federation of 50 legally independent states. The 48 contiguous states cover an area of 2,700 miles from east to west coasts, and 1,350 miles from north to south borders. The other two states are Alaska, bordering northwest Canada, and Hawaii, a group of islands in the Pacific. Other U.S. possessions include the territories of Puerto Rico, Guam, American Samoa, and the Virgin Islands. The bordering nations of Canada and Mexico are additional, relatively accessible markets. The U.S. has 169 cities with a population of 100,000 or more. (See Major Regional Markets in Exhibit 2).

History

During the 16th to 18th centuries, a group of 13 colonies congregated along the Atlantic seaboard, gained independence from England in 1776, and adopted the U.S. Constitution to establish the fledgling nation. After a disastrous civil war, the late 1800s were dedicated to rehabilitation and expansion, with pioneering efforts in the western territories extending to the Pacific Ocean. The 20th century is witness to a world power with a large and stable economy.

Government

The U.S. government is a republic. The 1787 Constitution established a delicate balance of power among the executive, legislative, and judiciary branches. There are two main political parties – the Democratic and Republican parties – which control national, state, and local elected offices. All those above the age of 18 are eligible to vote according to their choice.

The executive branch, headed by a president elected every four years, is responsible for enforcing the laws passed by the legislature. With the advice and consent of the Senate, the president, who is also the commander-in-chief of the military, can make treaties and appoint ambassadors, executive department officers, and federal court judges.

The legislative branch is composed of a Congress divided into two separate bodies: the House of Representatives and the Senate. The House is composed of more than 400 current seats, allocated among the states based on population. Members are elected to a two-year term by popular vote of citizens within specified voting districts. The Senate is composed of two senators elected from each state. Members are elected to six-year terms, with one-third changing every two years. Both the House and the Senate must pass all legislation by majority, which also requires

Exhibit 2 **MAJOR REGIONAL MARKETS**

Northeast:
  New England:
    Maine
    New Hampshire
    Vermont
    Massachusetts
    Rhode Island
    Connecticut

  Mid-Atlantic
    New York
    New Jersey
    Pennsylvania

Midwest:
  East North Central:
    Ohio
    Indiana
    Illinois
    Michigan
    Wisconsin

  West North Central:
    Minnesota
    Iowa
    Missouri
    North Dakota
    South Dakota
    Nebraska
    Kansas
South:
  South Atlantic:
    Delaware
    Maryland
    Washington, D.C.
    Virginia
    West Virginia
    North Carolina
    South Carolina
    Georgia
    Florida

East South Central:
  Kentucky
  Tennessee
  Alabama
  Mississippi

West South Central:
  Arkansas
  Louisiana
  Oklahoma
  Texas

West:
  Mountain:
    Montana
    Idaho
    Wyoming
    Colorado
    New Mexico
    Arizona
    Utah
    Nevada

  Pacific:
    Washington
    Oregon
    California
    Alaska
    Hawaii

Source: U.S. Department of Commerce

presidential approval. A presidential veto can, however, be overruled by a two-thirds majority of both House and Senate.

The Supreme Court has the judicial power, with ultimate appellate jurisdiction over both law and fact in reviewing decisions of other courts. District courts have jurisdiction in all matters of federal law, controversies between states, or citizens of different or foreign states, subject to appellate court review. There are also other courts, for specialized matters, including the Tax, Patent, Claims, and Customs Courts. Federal judges are appointed for life, and can be removed for misconduct.

Each state has a written constitution providing for a chief executive (governor), legislature, and a judicial system, similar to the federal system.

Other facts

English is the national language. The recent influx of immigrants from Latin American countries has swelled the percentage of the population speaking Spanish, particularly in the Southwest.

There are four time zones – Eastern, Central, Mountain, and Pacific, resulting in a three-hour time difference between New York City and Los Angeles. Hawaii lies an additional three hours to the west. Most of the country uses "daylight savings time" from April to October, advancing the clock one hour.

Several attempts to convert to the metric system for the U.S. have failed, and it is not likely that this will change in the near future. The chart of measurements is as follows:

Weights
16 ounces (oz) = 1 pound (lb)

2000 lbs = 1 ton

Distances
12 inches (in) = 1 foot (ft)

3 ft = 1 yard (yd)
1760 yds = 1 mile

Surface
4840 sq. yds = 1 acre

Volume
16 fluid oz = 1 pint (pt)
2 pts = 1 quart (qt)
4 qts = 1 gallon (gal)

Temperature
0 deg. Centigrade = 32 deg. Farenheit
100 deg. C = 212 deg. F
Conversion formula: TK

1 oz = 28.35 g
1 lb = 0.454 kg
1 ton = .907 metric ton

1 in = 2.54 cm
1 ft = 0.305 m
1 yd = 0.914 m
1 mile = 1.609 km

1 acre = 0.405 hectare

1 fl. oz. = 29.57 ml
1 pt = 0.473 l
1 qt = 0.946 l
1 gal = 3.785 l

2. Business entities

General commercial law

Under the federal system, both federal and state governments share governmental powers. In certain areas, activities such as interstate commerce (shipments or activities crossing state lines) are subject to both federal and state laws. Foreign capital is treated in much the same manner as domestic capital. Investments from abroad, including the acquisition of U.S. business by foreign persons, are not generally restricted, except in regulated industries such as aviation, banking, insurance, utilities, and in some cases, farmland.

Because of all the reporting requirements – especially federal – applying to owning property or acquiring domestic businesses, foreign companies intending to do business in the U.S. should obtain competent legal counsel.

Forms of business enterprise

U.S. law permits various forms of business organization, primarily sole proprietorships, partnerships (general or limited), and corporations. There is no federal business corporation law, and each state has its own laws and regulations for forming businesses and establishing proprietorships, partnerships, and branch offices. Establishing a branch requires only registration with state and municipality.

Corporations

A corporation can be established in any state, regardless of the location of its plant or facilities in the U.S. Various factors, including state taxes, determine the selection of the state of incorporation. Once it is established in one state, a company can conduct business in any other state, subject to registration of substantial activities such as establishing offices. Complying is a simple, inexpensive legal procedure.

When establishing a corporation in the U.S., a company must file articles of incorporation and by-laws stating:

- the name of the corporation;
- its place of business;
- the object of the enterprise;
- its projected lifespan (can be unlimited);
- the amount of authorized capital stock;
- other information pertaining to structure and operations.

While day-to-day responsibility rests with management, the board of directors is responsible for overall management of the company. Stockholders elect the directors, and the board then typically appoints a president, one or more vice presidents, a treasurer, and a secretary. Large corporations have several levels of vice presidents, including senior and executive, responsible for areas such as finance, operations, communications, information systems, and human resources. Directors and officers need not be citizens or residents of the U.S. In respect to employee participation, there are no legal requirements for employees to be represented on a company's board of directors, or for employers to establish profit-sharing plans.

The corporation's by-laws grant the officers their authority, in accordance with the statutes of the state of incorporation. By law, companies must generally have at least one annual shareholders' meeting. This can be waived for certain privately owned companies, depending on the state of incorporation. While incorporation costs vary from state to state, they are nominal in amount and should not affect the decision of whether or not to incorporate. Once the decision is made, companies should retain legal counsel to prepare the various documents and filings.

Joint ventures

Joint ventures are organized as a partnership of individuals, corporations, or both.

3. Employment

Availability of labor

About 47% of the U.S. population (approximately 114 million persons) compose the available labor pool. About 7% of this pool remained unemployed in 1987. In contrast to many other countries, workers in the U.S. are responsive to opportunities which require relocation. This mobility facilitates finding and employing an adequate work force.

Employer/employee relations

In 1981, gross hourly earnings, including overtime, averaged approximately $8.00 per hour for all occupations.

There are several federal benefit programs protecting employees:

- *Social security:* covers virtually all employees, providing retirement and disability benefits. Costs are shared equally by employer and employee. Combined rate of participation in 1987 was 14.3% of the first $43,800 earned.

- *Unemployment compensation:* varies from state to state, generally averaging 2.7% of the first $7,000 earned.

The standard work week is 40 hours, over five days, with overtime being paid at a percentage of the regular hourly rate.

Federal law makes it illegal to discriminate on the grounds of sex, race, nationality, or religion, in employment, training, and related matters. In addition to the federal programs and regulations, some states have their own employment and protection requirements.

Trade unions

The 230 or so U.S. labor unions represent some 20% of the total labor force, varying significantly by industry and region. They constitute an important aspect of employer/employee relations, and should be considered when choosing locations. They are usually organized into 'locals' and serve to negotiate with management on collective contracts for the employees. They do not represent company or plant management, and, in general, their officials don't participate in management decisions.

The dominant labor union is the American Federation of Labor (AFL-CIO), which represents the trucking and shipping industries.

Non-union companies are not required to establish employment contracts. However, they usually have certain personnel policies made known to employees when they are hired. Strikes in the U.S., while not common, do take place from time to time but cause a minimal loss of working time and productivity.

Other benefits

Most employment arrangements, union or non-union, provide for:

- *Holidays:* Most companies observe between six and eight holidays per year, for which employees receive basic pay. Companies may also observe state, local, and other holidays.
- *Vacation:* While there is no legal requirement to grant a paid period of leave, most companies grant one to four weeks' paid vacations, depending on level of employment, years of service, etc.
- *Healthcare and life insurance:* Employer and employee usually share the insurance costs, with reduced rate premiums for group plans.
- *Pension plans:* Employer-maintained plans cover about 25% of the work force, through voluntary or contractual agreements supplementing social security retirement payments.

It is customary to give employees whose employment is terminated a two-week notice, or more, if specified in the terms of employment.

Pensions

As mentioned above, social security is funded by both employee and employer contributions. Eligibility and the amount of benefits depend on the individual's earnings and number of years of contribution to the plan. The basic plan provides for:

- monthly benefit, beginning at age 62 minimum, for reduced benefits, and age 65 for full benefits;
- disability benefits under certain circumstances;
- death benefits to dependents;
- certain medical coverages.

Companies are not required to provide supplementary profit-sharing or retirement programs, although many do have them.

Insurance

Most companies insure plant, property, and equipment, and liability exposure. Insurance has cycles, and from time to time, liability coverage becomes a problem. Currently, there are some problems due to expensive and increasing damage awards. Alternatives such as risk management are becoming more popular.

4. Work permits

A foreign worker must obtain a visa in order to become employed in the U.S. Such visas are issued on two basic categories: immigrants and nonimmigrants. Immigrants are those who wish to enter the U.S. on a permanent basis. Visas for these individuals are usually more difficult to obtain and are generally allocated in accordance with a system of preferences based on annual quotas which usually are between one and two years. Nonimmigrant visas are for temporary periods. These visas are issued by U.S. consular offices at U.S. embassies and consular posts worldwide. While there are numerous categories of nonimmigrant visa classifications, the classifications used most often by foreign business people are the following:

- *B-1 visas (temporary business visitors)*
  This visa is issued to an alien visiting the U.S. for brief and limited business activity on behalf of a foreign employer. Such visas are issued for an initial period not exceeding six months and may be extended for an additional six-month period.

- *E-1 and E-2 visas (treaty traders and investors)*
  Where a treaty of friendship, commerce and navigation exists between the U.S. and certain countries, an E-1 or E-2 visa may be issued. E-1 visas are for the sole purpose of carrying on trade between the U.S. and the foreigner's home country. An E-2 visa is for the furtherance of a business venture in which the foreigner or the foreign employer has a substantial capital investment. These visas are issued for an initial period of one year and may be renewed for additional periods of two years indefinitely.

- *H visa (temporary employees or trainees)*
  These visas may be granted to foreigners coming to the U.S. to perform a particular service or to be trained in methods that will be used in a foreign country.

- *L-1 visa (intra-company transferee)*
  L-1 visas are issued to foreign managers, executives or individuals with specialized knowledge and who have been employed by the foreign employer for at least one year abroad. This visa is ideal for an individual who will be sent to begin or to supervise a U.S. operation. The L-1 is issued for up to three years, subject to renewals for a total

period of five years. Under this visa, as well as the E-1, E-2 and H visas, the foreigner may receive payment for services from a U.S. source.

It should be noted that due to the complexity and timing of obtaining visas, legal advice should be sought and sufficient time should be given to allow for the issuance of the appropriate visa.

Part Two

Finance and Investment

5. Regulatory agencies

Regulation of business

Any company doing business in the U.S. is subject to regulations enacted by a number of agencies:

- Civil Service Commission;

- Consumer Product Safety Commission (CPSC);

- Environmental Protection Agency (EPA);

- Equal Employment Opportunity Commission (EEOC);

- Federal Trade Commission (FTC);

- National Labor Relations Board;

- Occupational Safety and Health Review Commission (OSHA);

- Securities and Exchange Commission (SEC).

Currently, the government has recognized that regulations impose heavy indirect taxes on production, increase risk, and lower investment. It has recently undertaken to reduce and consolidate existing regulations. Such deregulation has particularly affected the banking and transportation industries.

Antitrust and anticompetitive practices

Antitrust legislation protects the basic competitive environment in the U.S. It also protects the interests of the general public. There are no statutory price controls in the U.S., and antitrust and related statutes prohibit practices of price discrimination, restricted competition, and deceptive advertising. Competition from abroad by direct investment is consistent with this policy. The FTC and Antitrust Division of the Department of Justice are responsible for enforcing antitrust policies, and have assured and demonstrated that there will be no discrimination against foreign investors.

Price setting or collusion is strictly prohibited, by federal and state laws, and subject to heavy penalties.

Consumer and environmental protection

State and federal laws require that products be properly labeled. They must also have adequate quality controls to protect the public in matters of health and safety. The following federal agencies administer these laws:

Agency	Responsibility
Food and Drug Administration	Content and labeling of foods, drugs, cosmetic, and therapeutic devices
U.S. Department of Agriculture	Quality of meats, milk, and other food products
U.S. Transportation Department	Vehicle quality and safety
Federal Trade Commission	Labeling of non-food, non-drug products, and false advertising
Environmental Protection Agency	Prevention or elimination of pollution

States have their own environmental standards, enforced through voluntary compliance or court action when necessary. Prospective investors need to be familiar with these standards and can contact the individual states' environmental agencies for further information.

Import and export controls

The U.S. is a member of the General Agreement on Tariffs and Trade (GATT). It is committed to free international exchange of goods and services, and to reducing existing tariffs and other trade barriers.

The U.S. Bureau of Customs is responsible for monitoring imports. It is possible to obtain a binding ruling on tariff classification and rate of duty by supplying to the Commissioner of Customs a complete description of the goods imported, including cost of manufacture and intended use. From time to time, quotas limiting the quantity of certain imports are imposed to protect domestic industry.

Exports are free of duties and proceeds freed of exchange controls, subject to U.S. foreign policy requirements on trade with certain countries.

Reporting requirements for foreign investors

The U.S. Department of Commerce, Bureau of Economic Analysis (BEA), has developed comprehensive reporting requirements to track certain foreigner activities in the U.S. The reports are for analyses and statistics.

They cannot be used for purposes of taxation, investigation, or regulation, and are immune from legal process. The following activities are tracked:

- acquisition of a 10% or more voting interest in a U.S. enterprise by a foreign person;
- acquisition of a U.S. business enterprise by an affiliate of a foreign person that has merged into the affiliate;
- acquisition of real estate by a foreign person for business purposes, no matter what the size;
- transactions between a U.S. affiliate and its foreign parent;
- formation of a new affiliate;
- creation of a joint venture between a U.S. and foreign person;
- total acquisitions during a fiscal year of real estate and business interests by a foreign person.

Patents, trademarks, and copyrights

The U.S. Department of Commerce Bureau of Patents and Trademarks grants patents for 17 years, with exclusive rights to the holder. Trademarks are also registered with the Bureau of Patents and Trademarks for a renewable 20-year period. Generic terms cannot be registered, however.

Copyrights cover books, periodicals, lectures, sermons, plays, musical compositions, motion pictures, works of art, drawings, photographs, maps, models, and advertising. A copy or sample must be deposited with the Copyright Office. Books and periodicals must first be published, carry a copyright notice, and be filed (two copies) with the Library of Congress. Copyrights are valid for the life of the creator plus 50 years, or of a corporation, 75 years from the date of first publication. Theft of trade secrets, which are protected under U.S. law, raiding a competitor for key personnel, and industrial espionage are considered unfair methods of competition.

Exchange control

The general policy of the U.S. is to admit and treat foreign capital on the basis of equality with domestic capital. Foreign investors may transfer or repatriate their capital freely, invest anywhere in the U.S. and, with minor exceptions, in any industry. There are a few sensitive sectors of the economy (communications, airlines, shipping, mining on federal lands, and power generation) where, in accordance with accepted international custom, foreign investment is limited by law.

6. Banking and local finance

Sources and methods of financing

The U.S. has many sources of capital and credit. These include venture capital, private investors, commercial banks, investment banks or underwriters – which arrange most of the larger-issue, long-term financing – and institutional lenders. Foreign banks may conduct business in the specified 'free trade zones' – New York, San Francisco, Houston, and Miami – and can lend to foreign companies in these zones.

Banks

National banks receive their charter from, and are monitored by, the Comptroller of the Currency, U.S. Treasury Department. They must be members of the Federal Reserve System (an independent central banking authority controlling the supply of money and credit, holding banking system reserves, and regulating member banks) and the Federal Deposit Insurance Corporation (FDIC). State banks are organized under state law, and regulated and supervised by state banking authorities, similar to the national system. Most are members of the Federal Reserve System and FDIC, or have access to similar facilities.

Short-term financing

Commercial banks usually provide lines-of-credit, bankers' acceptances, or letters of credit for short-term financing, and may require security depending on the borrower's reputation and familiarity to the bank. Entities usually have substantial capital, supplemented by borrowings. Rates are based on the magnitude and type of borrowing, collateral, term and purpose of the loan, and balances maintained.

Interest rates vary depending on the 'prime rate' which fluctuates in response to the economy and the value of the dollar, among other factors. A bank's best customers can usually receive the prime rate; others pay a rate based on an agreed upon amount in excess of the prime rate.

Equipment and real estate leasing is available through a number of sources. While this can raise the cost of money, it can also provide additional liquidity and help conserve working capital.

Long-term financing

Institutional lenders – insurance companies and pension funds, provide long-term financing, usually for 10- to 20-year terms. By lending against real estate mortgages, for example, they provide funds for constructing and equipping business facilities. Interest rates are normally fixed at loan initiation, and remain constant. They depend on the borrower's credit rating, collateral, provisions for sinking funds or early redemption, and the lender's perception of future inflation. If bonds are sold to the general public, it is necessary to comply with federal and state securities laws.

Equity markets

Investment bankers and underwriters also arrange financing through equity securities (stock), sold to the general public in compliance with federal and state regulations. Shares of stock in U.S. corporations differ from those in most other countries as follows:

- U.S. corporate shares are registered in the name of the shareholder or designated nominee;
- A designation of par value is of little significance and bears no relevance to real value.

There are extensive secondary trading markets for both stocks and bonds, principally the New York Stock Exchange and the American Stock Exchange, and a broad over-the-counter market. Daily security trades are routinely reported in the newspapers.

Off-shore financing

An important source of off-shore financing for U.S. investors is the Eurodollar market. Eurodollar loans are available from commercial banks or Eurodollar bonds can be sold.

7. Accounts and audit requirements

Governance of financial reporting

Historically, financial reporting in the U.S. has been heavily regulated. As a result, the country has the most detailed and structured accounting and reporting requirements in the world. These requirements are developed by the various professional bodies (described below) and, for publicly held companies, by the Securities and Exchange Commission (SEC).

The Financial Accounting Standards Board (FASB), an independent organization, through the issuance of its Statements of Financial Accounting Standards (SFAS), is the predominant body responsible for establishing generally accepted accounting principles (GAAP) used in the preparation of financial statements.

Prior to the formation of the FASB, the American Institute of Certified Public Accountants (AICPA) was responsible for establishing GAAP. During that time, the AICPA issued a series of Accounting Principles Board Opinions and Accounting Research Bulletins. The AICPA is presently responsible for issuing Industry Audit Guides and other specialized accounting guidance.

The SEC administers the federal securities laws, including financial reporting rules and regulations. These laws include the Securities Act of 1933, governing the registration of securities to be sold in interstate public offerings, and the Securities Exchange Act of 1934, which deals with the periodic filing requirements of publicly held companies and the rules covering their applicable trading markets.

Statutory reporting requirements

There is no legal requirement for a privately owned company to prepare financial statements, unless the company operates in a regulated industry or the financial statements are required by an agreement (e.g. bank loan).

Companies registered with the SEC are required to file periodic reports and to notify the SEC as to significant developments. These periodic reports include:

- Form 10-K, the annual filing containing comparative audited financial statements, a comprehensive analysis by management of its financial condition and results of operations, and various other supplementary schedules. Form 10-K must be filed with the SEC within 90 days of a company's fiscal year-end;

- Form 10-Q, a report containing unaudited quarterly financial statements, to be filed with the SEC within 45 days after the end of each of a company's first three quarters;

- Form 8-K, a report describing significant events, such as acquisition of a business, to be filed with the SEC ordinarily within 15 days of the occurrence of the event.

In addition, public companies prepare annual stockholders' reports containing financial information similar to that included in Form 10-K.

Under certain conditions, foreign companies that seek to acquire a U.S. publicly traded company may be required to file financial and other information with the SEC and such information would also be available to the general public.

Books and records

Federal and state laws require entities to maintain books and records necessary to support the information shown in tax returns. In addition, record keeping requirements of certain industries (e.g. banking, insurance, securities brokerage) are regulated to some extent by both federal and state regulatory bodies.

Companies subject to SEC jurisdiction are required by law to:

- keep books and records, in reasonable detail, which accurately and fairly reflect the transactions and disposition of the company's assets;

- devise and maintain a system of internal accounting controls which will provide reasonable assurance that:

  — transactions are properly recorded in accordance with management's authorization;

  — financial statements are prepared in conformity with GAAP and accountability for assets is maintained;

  — Access to company assets is permitted only with management's authorization.

While there is no specific requirement as to where the books and records must be kept, normal practice is to maintain them at the company's principal place of business. For federal income tax purposes, books and records must be maintained for specified time periods, which may be longer under various state laws.

23

Auditors and audit requirements

Privately held companies are not required by law to have their financial statements audited. However, many of these companies are required by banks or other creditors to furnish audited financial statements. Furthermore, companies in certain industries (e.g. banking, insurance) supervised by government agencies, may be required to undergo an annual audit.

Publicly held companies registered with the SEC are required to file annual reports containing audited financial statements. Other publicly held companies ordinarily furnish shareholders with similar reports.

A company's independent auditors, who must either be certified public accountants or, less frequently, public accountants, are normally appointed by the company's management. In the case of publicly held companies, this appointment may be ratified by the shareholders.

Auditors are subject to strict independence rules prescribed by the AICPA and, in the case of SEC filing companies, by the SEC. These rules are intended to ensure that the auditor is independent in fact and appearance and is, therefore, in a position to issue an unbiased opinion on the financial statements. Direct and material indirect financial interests in clients are prohibited. Bookkeeping services may be provided to privately held companies only, without impairing independence, provided the services are not tantamount to making management decisions.

The auditor's report, based on reporting standards established by the AICPA, should state whether, in the auditor's opinion, the financial statements and notes are presented fairly in conformity with GAAP consistently applied.

In certain circumstances, the auditor may be unable to render an unqualified opinion on the financial statements. In these situations, either a qualified or adverse opinion would be issued or the auditor may disclaim an opinion. In a qualified report, a separate explanatory paragraph should be included, explaining the reasons for the qualification. The SEC will generally not accept an auditor's report which is qualified as to either audit scope or the accounting principles used.

Some companies which do not require or desire audits may engage an accountant to perform review or compilation services instead. A review provides negative assurance that the accountant is not aware of any material modifications that should be made to the financial statements in order for them to be in conformity with GAAP. On the other hand, in a compilation, an accountant is only involved in the preparation of financial statements, and no assurances are given on the financial statements.

Accounting profession

The accounting profession essentially is self-regulated, although CPAs must be licensed by the states in which they practice and, as such, are governed by various state ethics rules. The principal professional accounting body is the AICPA, which is responsible for establishing rules on professional ethics, auditing, and reporting standards applicable to its members. Virtually all practicing CPAs in major accounting firms, and most other CPAs, are members of the AICPA.

Auditing standards

The standards required to be followed by auditors are established by the AICPA as 'Statements on Auditing Standards', which are normally more comprehensive than those of most other countries. In addition, many accounting firms have internal standards that may impose stricter standards on its personnel than those required by the profession.

Form and content of financial statements

The form and content of financial statements of most privately held companies are governed by professional standards established by the FASB and AICPA. Generally there are no statutory requirements. Publicly held companies and companies in certain regulated industries, however, are governed by their applicable regulatory body (e.g. the SEC).

Financial statements should be prepared in accordance with GAAP. Under GAAP, a company's financial statements should contain, at a minimum, the following:

- balance sheet;
- income statement;
- statement of changes in stockholders' equity (required if there have been changes other than in retained earnings);
- statement of changes in financial position (to be replaced by a statement of cash flows for years ending after July 15, 1988);
- notes to financial statements (including a summary of accounting policies followed by the company).

Publicly held companies are required to present their financial statements in comparative form. This is also general practice for other companies. The contents of the financial statements, including the footnotes, are the responsibility of management, regardless of who has actually prepared them or whether they are audited. If the financial statements are audited, non-compliance with GAAP will generally result in either a qualified or an adverse auditor's opinion.

Company law of certain foreign countries, such as the Directives of the European Economic Community, cause parent companies resident in the EEC to require that their U.S. subsidiaries maintain their books and records in accordance with the foreign countries' requirements and to prepare their financial statements in accordance with the accounting principles followed by the parent. This is acceptable under U.S. standards. However, it should be noted that such subsidiaries may also need to comply with U.S. record keeping rules and may be required to prepare a separate set of financial statements in accordance with U.S. GAAP.

Group financial statements

Consolidated financial statements are generally required if a company controls more than 50% of the voting shares of another company unless control is likely to be temporary. In determining whether consolidation is appropriate, the goal should be to provide the most meaningful financial presentation in the circumstances. In effect, substance should prevail over form.

The FASB has adopted rules which require consolidation of non-homogeneous subsidiaries for years ending after December 15, 1988.

Where control does not exist, but the investor has significant influence over the investee (usually between 20 and 50% of the investee's voting shares), the investment should be accounted for by the equity method. The investment is initially recorded at cost and is subsequently adjusted for the investor's proportionate share of the investee's profits or losses.

When there is no significant influence, the investment should be accounted for under the cost method, where the investor does not record its share of the investee's profits or losses, but records as income any dividends from the investee.

Subsidiaries' year-ends should ordinarily coincide with that of the parent. Where there are different year-ends (up to three months is acceptable for SEC filing companies), appropriate disclosures should be made.

Valuation of assets

Financial statements ordinarily are based on historical cost. Upward revaluation of assets is generally not permitted. Acquired assets are generally stated at their original cost and depreciated or amortized over their estimated useful lives. Certain assets (e.g. inventories, marketable equity securities) are stated at the lower of their cost or estimable realizable value. In some cases, discounting of assets and liabilities may be appropriate to reflect the present value of future cash flow. The basis of valuing assets should be disclosed.

Footnotes

Companies must disclose the accounting policies followed for the more significant transactions and methods of valuation. Such items normally include revenue recognition, inventory valuation, depreciation and amortization methods for fixed and intangible assets, treatment of goodwill and other intangible assets, long-term contracts, related party transactions, income taxes, long-term debt, foreign currency translation methods and consolidation principles.

Publicly held companies are required by the SEC to provide certain additional disclosures.

Book and tax differences

Companies are required to provide for federal, state and local income taxes in their financial statements based on pretax accounting income. Determining the income tax provision is often complicated by frequent differences between financial income and taxable income. These differences may be either reversed in future years ("timing differences") or are permanent in nature. Deferred taxes are provided on timing differences (called "temporary differences" under a new FASB rule effective in 1989).

Deferred taxes are to be provided in all material timing differences and should be reflected in the balance sheet as a deferred credit or charge.

8. Exchange controls

There are no exchange controls imposed on the remittance of profits and repatriation of capital, except that repatriation of capital, controlled directly or indirectly, by North Korea, Vietnam, Cambodia and Cuba or nationals of these countries, regardless of their place of residence, is not permitted without a Treasury Department license.

9. Restrictions on foreign investment

Government attitude towards foreign investment

At the federal level, there are generally no restrictions on foreign investment in the U.S. Normally, there also are no restrictions imposed by the states. However, in those cases where foreign countries impose restrictions, some states impose similar restrictions on investors from such countries.

Investments by foreigners are restricted only in certain industries, including:

- domestic radio communications;
- coastal or fresh water shipping;
- domestic air transportation;
- hydroelectric power;
- use of nuclear materials.

Reporting requirements of foreign investors

Foreign investors are required to meet certain federal reporting and disclosure requirements. These include requirements under the Tax Equity and Fiscal Responsibility Act of 1982 (TEFRA), the Foreign Investment in Real Property Tax Act of 1980 (FIRPTA), the International Survey Act of 1976 (ISA), and the Agricultural Foreign Investment Disclosure Act of 1978 (AFIDA).

Under the ISA, the U.S. Department of Commerce is to obtain information concerning foreign investments in U.S. business enterprises. There are two sets of forms required to be filed in these circumstances. The first relates to an acquisition or formation of a U.S. business meeting certain size tests. The second is required to be filed periodically by the U.S. investee. Such information is confidential and is limited to use by the U.S. government for analytical and statistical purposes. Normally, U.S. professional advisors (e.g. accountants and lawyers) will be able to advise the foreign investor about such requirements.

AFIDA requires most acquisitions or transfers of any interest by a foreign person in agricultural land to be reported to the Department of Agriculture.

Part Three

The Tax System

10. The tax structure

Taxing authorities

Taxes are levied by the federal, state, and local governments. The federal tax law is set forth in the Internal Revenue Code of 1986 and its predecessors, enacted and amended by Congress. The Treasury Department issues interpretive regulations and administers the federal law through the Internal Revenue Service (IRS).

Principal taxes

Taxes on income and gains:

Corporation income tax
Individual income tax
Income tax on trusts and estates
Environmental tax on corporations

Taxes on transactions:

Sales and use tax
Excise tax
Customs duties

Taxes on transfers of wealth:

Gift tax
Estate tax
Generation skipping transfer tax
Inheritance tax

Taxes on property:

Real property
Personal property

Taxes on payroll:

Federal insurance contributions (social security)
Unemployment tax

Income tax structure

Under the U.S. system, the federal government taxes all income which does not fall within one of the specific exclusions set out in the Internal Revenue Code. States which impose income taxes, or corporate franchise taxes based on income, also tax all income unless it is specifically excluded by the state's tax statute or the U.S. Constitution.

Income taxes are imposed on corporations, individuals, trusts, and estates. The federal rates are progressive. Some states tax at a flat rate while others use progressive rates. Most corporations and estates may use either the calendar year or a fiscal year ending on the last day of any month as their tax year. The tax year of individuals, partnerships, and trusts generally must be the calendar year.

Federal tax rates

The federal tax consists of two components – the income tax and the alternative minimum tax.

The top corporate income rate is 34% for tax years beginning after June 30, 1987. The top income tax rate for individuals, trusts, and estates is 28% for tax years beginning after 1987, although the effective top rate after 1987 may reach 33% in some cases because of the phase-out of the lower tax-bracket amounts and personal exemptions. Capital gains are included in taxable income in the same way as any other income.

The purpose of the alternative minimum tax is to ensure that all taxpayers with substantial economic income pay at least some tax. The rate is 20% for corporations and 21% for other taxpayers. It is imposed on taxable income plus specified tax preferences, and is paid to the extent it exceeds the income tax.

International aspects

Domestic corporations and U.S. citizens and residents are subject to tax on their worldwide income. Foreign corporations and nonresident aliens are taxed at the same rates as domestic entities on income effectively connected with the conduct of a U.S. trade or business. In addition, the U.S. imposes a tax on the U.S. branch profits of a foreign corporation, unless the profits are reinvested in the U.S.

U.S. source fixed or determinable annual or periodical income paid to foreigners, such as interest, dividends, rents, and royalties, is subject to tax at a flat 30% (or lower treaty rate) if this income is not effectively connected with the conduct of a U.S. trade or business. Interest paid by banks, savings institutions, and insurance companies generally is not subject to this 30% tax. The tax is withheld at source by the payor.

Interest on portfolio indebtedness issued after July 18, 1984 by U.S. borrowers (including the U.S. Treasury) is also exempt from the 30% tax. This exemption does not apply to interest paid to:

- 10% or more shareholders;
- controlled foreign corporations, if paid by related U.S. persons; and
- foreign banks pursuant to loan agreements entered into in the ordinary course of business.

Certain capital gains of foreign corporations and nonresident aliens are considered fixed or determinable income and subject to the flat 30% rate. Otherwise, capital gains which are not effectively connected with a U.S. trade or business are not subject to tax except in the case of a nonresident alien individual who is present in the U.S. for at least 183 days during the tax year.

The U.S. has an extensive network of tax treaties which reduce or eliminate the 30% flat tax on many forms of income. These treaties contain various provisions mitigating double taxation and require the treaty parties to appoint competent authorities to resolve disagreements. However, recourse to competent authority rarely is satisfactory.

Future developments

The U.S. tax structure constantly changes because of new legislation, regulations, rulings, and court decisions. This booklet generally does not cover developments after October 1987.

11. Administration

Federal taxes are administered and collected by the IRS, an agency of the U.S. Treasury Department. State and local taxes are administered and collected by the respective state and local tax departments.

Federal tax policy is proposed by the Treasury Department and the U.S. Congress, and enacted into law by Congress. State and local tax policies are proposed by the various state and local tax departments and their respective legislative bodies and enacted into law by the latter.

Since state and local administrative rules vary, the remaining discussion is confined to federal tax administration.

Corporate taxpayers

Compliance

The U.S. tax system is based on self-assessment. The taxpayer files a return reporting taxable income and computing the tax.

If the return is not filed by the due date (including extensions), the IRS may assess the tax, or begin a proceeding in court to collect the tax without assessment, any time after the due date.

Tax returns

The income tax return of a corporation is due on the 15th of the third month after the end of the tax year. An automatic six-month extension of time may be obtained by filing an application with the IRS.

The return must disclose all items of gross income and deductions. It must also show the corporation's balance sheet at the beginning and end of the tax year, and reconcile taxable income with book (financial statement) income. Foreign-controlled corporations must also submit Form 5472 disclosing information on transactions with related entities. U.S. persons owning 5% or more of a foreign corporation must file Form 5471 disclosing similar information.

Payroll tax reports generally are filed on a quarterly and/or annual basis, by the end of the month following the quarter or year.

Payment and collection

All payments of corporate income tax must be made to a financial institution which qualifies as a federal tax depositary. Advance estimated payments are due in four installments, on the 15th day of the 4th, 6th, 9th, and 12th months of the tax year. The balance of tax due must be paid by the 15th day of the third month after the end of the tax year.

The employer must remit income tax and federal insurance contributions (social security) withheld from salaries and wages, as well as the employer's share of federal insurance contributions, quarterly, monthly, or more frequently – depending upon the total amount of tax involved. Generally, these payments are also made by deposit with a qualified financial institution.

Tax audits

The IRS can assess additional tax within three years after the return is due, or after it is filed if filed late. A six-year assessment period applies if the taxpayer omits items of income which amount to more than 25% of the gross income reported in the return. There is an unlimited assessment period if fraud is involved, or if no return is filed. Ordinarily, assessments of additional tax result from audits of returns by the IRS. The process by which the IRS selects returns for audit is a closely guarded secret.

Appeal procedures

If the taxpayer does not agree with an assessment proposed by an auditor, a protest appealing the assessment may be filed with the IRS Appeals Office. Appeals to the IRS Appeals Office may be handled by CPAs, lawyers, or other agents admitted to practice before the Treasury Department. If agreement cannot be reached with the Appeals Office, the taxpayer may carry its case to the federal courts. A CPA may represent the taxpayer in the U.S. Tax Court, but only a lawyer may handle a case in other U.S. courts.

If a taxpayer believes its tax has been overpaid, it may claim relief by filing a refund claim within three years from the time the return was due or filed (if later), or within two years after paying the tax. If the claim is rejected by the IRS, the taxpayer may pursue the issue in the IRS Appeals Office and the federal courts.

Most tax treaties provide for appeals to competent authority, but such appeals are expensive and time consuming.

Non-corporate taxpayers

Compliance and returns

Noncorporate taxpayers include individuals, estates, and trusts. In general, the compliance requirements for noncorporate taxpayers are similar to those for corporations. Taxpayers must file annual returns of income, which generally are due on the 15th day of the fourth month after the tax year ends. Individuals may obtain an automatic four-month extension of this due date by filing an application with the IRS. A further two-month extension may be granted by the IRS upon request. Estates and trusts may request extensions of up to six months for filing their returns.

Withholding on wages and salaries

Tax on income from employment is collected by deduction at source by the employer. When employment begins, the employee must give his employer an Employee's Withholding Allowance Certificate (Form W-4) which sets forth the withholding allowances which the employee is entitled to claim based on his deductions and credits. This certificate must be resubmitted when these allowances change. New certificates also may be required if there is a major change in the tax law.

The employer is required to deduct the appropriate income tax from each payment of remuneration, based on tables issued by the IRS which take into account the allowances claimed on Form W-4. The employer holds the amounts withheld as trust funds and must remit them to the IRS at the prescribed time.

Payment and collection

Withholding at source does not relieve an employee of the obligation to file a return. In addition, although the withholding system is designed to arrive at the correct amount of tax, it does not work perfectly, and the tax withheld may exceed or be less than the actual tax due. Further, many taxpayers receive income that is not subject to withholding.

Any tax due in excess of the amount withheld must be estimated and paid in advance to the IRS, generally in four installments. These installments are due on the 15th day of the fourth, sixth, and ninth months of the tax year and on the 15th day of the first month after the tax year ends. The balance of tax due, if any, must be paid to the IRS by the 15th day of the fourth month after the tax year ends. Penalties may be assessed if less than 90% of the final tax is paid through withholding and estimated payments.

Foreign personnel

Foreign nationals resident in the U.S. are subject to the same compliance requirements as U.S. citizens.

Exit permits

Departing aliens must declare their income tax liability and obtain a certificate from the director of the local IRS district. This certificate must state that the alien has complied with all of the obligations imposed upon him by the income tax laws. The certificate, or evidence that no certificate is necessary, must be presented at the point of departure. Certificates are not required for:

- foreign diplomats, their families, and servants;
- alien students and industrial trainees;
- certain aliens visiting for pleasure or business;
- certain aliens in transit;
- certain aliens admitted to the U.S. on border-crossing identification cards;
- alien military trainees; or
- alien residents of Canada or Mexico who frequently commute to the U.S. for employment and whose wages are subject to withholding.

Part Four

Taxes on Business

12. Corporate tax system

In general

Domestic corporations are subject to tax on their worldwide income. Foreign corporations are taxable only on U.S. source income. A domestic corporation is a corporation organized or created under the laws of the U.S., any state or territory, or the District of Columbia. A foreign corporation is any corporation which is not a domestic corporation.

Taxable entities

The term "corporation" may include an unincorporated association which has the characteristics of a corporation. However, it excludes a partnership. A corporate member of a partnership is subject to tax on its share of the partnership's profits. The treatment of partnerships is dealt with on page 58.

Certain "small business corporations" can elect to be treated for tax purposes in a manner similar to partnerships. A small business corporation is a domestic corporation, with only one class of stock. It may not have more than 35 shareholders. These shareholders must be citizens, resident aliens, estates, or specified types of trusts. A small business corporation must not own 80% or more of another corporation. Certain types of corporations are not eligible to make this election. A corporation which makes this election is known as an "S corporation".

Accounting periods and methods

Taxable income is ascertained separately for each tax year. A tax year cannot exceed 12 months and must end on the last day of a month. Normally, the corporation uses the same tax year as its fiscal year for financial statement purposes. S corporations are generally required to use the calendar year.

A company's taxable income is determined on the basis of accounts prepared on the historical cost basis. Specific statutory adjustments are made to the accounting profits to arrive at taxable income. Transactions with related parties, including foreign affiliates, at other than arm's-length prices or rates can be adjusted for tax purposes by the IRS.

All non-farm business taxpayers must use the accrual method of accounting if inventories are a material income-producing factor. If inventories are not involved, S corporations and corporations whose average annual gross receipts do not exceed $5 million for the three previous tax years may use the cash method. Income from long-term contracts may be reported under special rules.

Gross income

Gross income includes gross profits from the sale of merchandise and other property which must be inventoried.

Inventory valuation

Any method of valuation of inventory (stock-in-trade and work in process) which is not specifically prohibited by the tax law and accords with sound commercial accounting principles is acceptable, provided that it is used consistently at the beginning and end of the tax year. However, the amounts of overhead which must be included in the inventory costs of manufacturers and sellers are prescribed by law and extensive IRS regulations. Inventory may be valued at cost, or at the lower of cost or market (replacement cost). Reserves for anticipated future losses may not be deducted.

Inventory costs may be computed under either the first-in first-out (FIFO) or last-in first-out (LIFO) methods. If the LIFO method is elected, inventory may be valued only at cost – the lower of cost or market method may not be used. The method selected must be used consistently. The taxpayer may change from the FIFO method to the LIFO method without permission, but a change from LIFO to FIFO requires IRS consent. The LIFO method may be used only if the same method is used for financial reporting purposes.

Capital gains

Capital gains are taxed at the same rate as ordinary income for tax years beginning after June 30, 1987. Capital losses are deductible only against capital gains. Unused capital losses generally are carried back three years and forward five years and deducted against any capital gains for those years. There are relief provisions for:

- exchanges of stock or securities in connection with corporate reorganizations;
- exchanges of certain other investments or business property; and
- involuntary conversions of property.

Interest

Interest is taxable in the year in which it is accrued or received. Any foreign income tax withheld may be deducted or used as a credit against the corporation's income tax. Interest earned on most obligations of state and local governments is exempt from federal taxation. The states are prohibited from taxing interest on U.S. obligations, but they usually tax interest derived from state and local government obligations other than their own.

Dividends

Dividends are includible in income in the year in which they are received. A corporate shareholder generally may deduct 70% of dividends included in income which are received from a taxable domestic corporation. The deduction is 80% if the corporation is 20% or more owned, and all dividends received from certain 80% or more owned domestic corporations are deductible.

Dividends received from a foreign corporation may qualify for the dividends received deduction. The deduction is available only to the extent the dividend represents income realized from a trade or business carried on in the U.S. by the foreign corporation. The corporate shareholder must own at least 10% (by vote and value) of the foreign corporation's stock.

Dividends paid are not deductible except in specialized cases, such as regulated investment companies and mutual insurance companies.

If foreign income tax is withheld on a dividend, it may be deducted as a tax or used as a credit against the shareholder's U.S. income tax.

A domestic corporation owning 10% or more of a foreign corporation's voting stock may claim a credit against its U.S. income tax for income taxes paid by the foreign corporation to a foreign country (or U.S. possession). This credit is the same proportion of the taxes paid by the foreign corporation as the dividends received are of the corporation's undistributed earnings. Different methods of computation are required depending on the year in which the earnings were accumulated. The tax claimed as a credit must be included in taxable income by "grossing up" the net dividend received.

Royalties

Royalties constitute taxable income. Any foreign income tax withheld may be deducted or used as a credit against the corporation's U.S. income tax.

Management fees

Management and service fees are taxable when accrued or received, depending on the taxpayer's method of accounting. Management fees received for services performed in the U.S. are U.S. source income, even if performed for a foreign entity.

Deductions

Depreciation

The allowable deduction for depreciation (cost recovery) of capital (fixed) assets used in the trade or business is computed using specific rates fixed by law, regardless of the amount charged in the accounts of the business.

Amortization

The cost of intangible personal property which has a limited life, such as patents, copyrights or contracts, may be recovered through amortization deductions over the property's life. A company may elect to amortize its organizational (formation) and business start-up expenses over sixty months. Costs of intangibles which have an indefinite life, such as goodwill, trademarks, or tradenames, are not amortizable. Their costs may be written off only when they are abandoned, become worthless, or are sold.

Interest expense

Interest generally is deductible when it is accrued or paid, depending on the accounting method. However, interest is not deductible if it is incurred to purchase or carry tax-exempt securities.

If an obligation is issued for the sale of property, additional interest income to the seller and interest expense to the buyer must be recognized if the contractual interest is less than the minimum prescribed by the IRS. The cost of the property is correspondingly reduced. Interest paid to related parties on borrowings is subject to arm's-length standards prescribed by IRS regulations. Additional income and expense on loans to employees, shareholders, and other specified persons may be imputed if interest is not based on IRS tables. The IRS may disallow a deduction claimed for interest if the payor has a high debt/equity ratio.

Employee remuneration

Remuneration for personal services is deductible if it is an ordinary and necessary business expense and reasonable in amount. Remuneration related to the cost of construction or acquisition of capital assets must be capitalized as part of asset cost.

Employee benefits

In addition to direct payments of remuneration, employers may deduct the costs of employee benefits, including retirement plans, health, accident, and group life insurance, worker's compensation for on-the-job injuries, and other fringe benefits. The Internal Revenue Code contains many detailed rules defining the terms under which these benefits are deductible.

Insurance premiums

Insurance premiums are deductible if they are incurred in connection with the corporation's trade or business. Life insurance premiums are not deductible if the corporation is a direct or indirect beneficiary of the insurance policy. Also not deductible are amounts added to self-insurance reserves. Premiums paid to a captive insurance company are deductible only if there is effective shifting of the risk of loss.

Bad debts

All businesses may deduct specific debts which become wholly or partially worthless. Certain financial institutions lending money for residential mortgages and certain small banks may deduct reasonable additions to a reserve for bad debts.

Advertising

A deduction is allowable for advertising expenses which reasonably relate to the corporation's business. However, advertising is not deductible if its purpose is to promote or defeat legislation.

Other deductions

The following are among the more common types of deductions:

- charitable contributions (limited to 10% of taxable income computed without this deduction – unused deductions may be carried forward for five years);

- depletion;
- rents;
- repairs;
- royalties; and
- taxes (excluding US income taxes and certain penalty taxes).

Net operating losses

Losses from business operations may be offset against income of any type (including capital gains) arising in the same tax year. Any net operating loss is carried back to reduce taxable income for the prior three years. Any balance of the loss may be deducted from taxable income earned in the next 15 years. A corporation may elect to waive the carryback of a loss and only carry it forward. Special provisions expedite the refunding of the tax reductions resulting from loss carrybacks.

The use of net operating loss carryovers is limited if there is an ownership change in the loss corporation within a three-year testing period. An ownership change occurs if the percentage of stock owned by one or more 5% shareholders in the loss corporation increases by more than 50 percentage points over the lowest percentage of stock owned in the loss corporation during the testing period. Similar rules apply to corporations which succeed to net operating losses because of corporate reorganizations.

The loss carryover is disallowed if the ownership of the loss corporation changes and the corporation does not continue the same business enterprise for two years after the ownership change.

Non-deductible items

Expenditures which are not deductible from taxable income include:

- any expenditure which is not an ordinary and necessary business expense;
- capital expenditures such as improvements to business premises, legal costs connected with the acquisition of capital assets, and expenses of raising capital; and
- general reserves against anticipated future losses.

Entertainment expenses are not deductible unless they are directly related to, or associated with, the active conduct of the corporation's trade or business. No deduction is permitted for the cost of entertainment facilities, such as resorts and hunting lodges. Business gifts exceeding $25 per donee generally are not deductible. Special rules apply to employee achievement awards.

Tax computation

Taxable income is the sum of all gross income, including capital gains, from which is subtracted the total of all allowable deductions. The gross tax liability is computed by applying the corporate tax rates to taxable income. Corporate tax rates effective July 1, 1987 are:

Taxable income	Tax rate
Not over $50,000	15%
Amount over $50,000 but not over $75,000	25%
Amount over $75,000	34%

A corporation with taxable income in excess of $100,000 pays an additional tax of 5% of income. This surtax may not exceed $11,750. The effect is that corporations with income in excess of $335,000 pay tax at a flat rate of 34%.

Tax credits

Credits against the gross tax liability are allowed for the following:

- *Foreign taxes paid on foreign source income*
  This credit is limited to the same ratio of the U.S. tax as the foreign source income is to worldwide taxable income. The limitation is applied separately to each of nine categories of income. The major categories are investment (passive) income, high withholding tax (5% or more) interest, financial services income, and operating income. Special rules apply to income received from more than 50% U.S.-owned foreign corporations.

  Any foreign income tax paid or accrued which exceeds the credit limitation may be carried back for two years and carried over for five years.

  A U.S. corporation which receives a dividend from a foreign corporation of which it owns at least 10% of the voting stock may claim a foreign tax credit for the taxes paid by the foreign corporation attributable to the dividend.

- *Research credit*
  A credit is available for incremental research expenses paid or incurred before 1989. The credit equals 20% of the increase in the amount of qualified research expenses paid or incurred in the current tax year over the average qualified research expenses for the three immediately preceding tax years. A 20% credit also is allowed for basic research payments to colleges, universities, research institutions, and certain other tax-exempt organizations, which exceed a special base amount.

49

This credit is limited to the first $25,000 of tax plus 75% of the tax exceeding $25,000. Any excess credit may be carried back three years and forward 15 years.

- *Targeted jobs credit*
  Employers hiring individuals from nine categories of disadvantaged groups may claim this credit. The credit equals 40% of the first $6,000 of first-year wages. The deduction for these wages must be reduced by the amount of the credit. The credit may not be claimed for wages paid to employees hired after 1988.

  The credit is limited to the first $25,000 of tax plus 75% of the tax exceeding $25,000. Any excess credit may be carried back three years and forward 15 years.

Alternative minimum tax

Corporations are subject to an alternative minimum tax (AMT) of 20% which is applied to the AMT base. The AMT is paid only to the extent it exceeds the income tax.

The AMT base is taxable income plus tax preferences less a $40,000 exemption. This exemption is phased out for higher-income corporations. The phase-out is equal to 25c for each $1 of AMT taxable income exceeding $150,000. The exemption is completely phased out when AMT taxable income reaches $310,000.

The more common corporate preferences are:

- excess book income;
- excess depreciation;
- deferred income from certain installment sales;
- deferred profit on some long-term contracts; and
- bad debt reserves of financial institutions.

The excess book income preference is 50% of the excess of the net income reported in the financial statements (with some adjustments) over AMT income (before adding this preference).

Depreciation on assets placed in service after 1986 generally is computed under the Modified Accelerated Cost Recovery System (MACRS) for regular tax purposes and under the Alternative Depreciation System (ADS) for AMT purposes. ADS usually generates lower depreciation than MACRS. The difference is a preference added to the AMT base. Accelerated depreciation on real property and leased personal property placed in service before 1987 also is a tax preference.

A net operating loss generally may be carried back three years and forward fifteen years for both income tax and AMT purposes. The AMT net operating loss must be computed separately, using AMT rules. A net operating loss is fully deductible against taxable income for tax purposes. For AMT purposes, only 90% of a net operating loss deduction may be used.

Generally, the only credit allowed against the AMT is the foreign tax credit. However, this credit can offset only 90% of the tentative AMT (computed without any net operating loss deduction). A limited amount of investment credit also may be available.

AMT paid on "deferral preferences" for prior years will be allowed as a credit against the income tax in a subsequent year to the extent this tax exceeds the tentative AMT in the subsequent year. Deferral preferences are all preferences except those that permanently reduce the income tax.

Related corporations

The Internal Revenue Code contains many intricate rules governing related corporations, which are designed to prevent tax avoidance through use of the corporate form. Corporations controlled by the same interests are called controlled groups. A controlled group may consist of a parent and subsidiary corporations and/or brother-sister corporations. Many corporate tax benefits and allowances available to a controlled group are restricted so as not to exceed those of a single corporation.

Consolidated income tax return

A parent-subsidiary group is known as an affiliated group. Members of an affiliated group may elect to file consolidated income tax returns. An affiliated group is a chain of corporations connected through 80% or more stock ownership with a common parent corporation. The 80% test requires stock ownership of 80% or more of both a subsidiary's voting power and value. Certain nonvoting and non-convertible preferred stock is ignored in calculating this 80% requirement. The following corporations may not be included in a consolidated return:

- life insurance companies;
- regulated investment companies;
- real estate investment trusts;
- tax-exempt corporations; and
- S corporations.

Advantages of filing consolidated returns

A consolidated return permits the affiliated group to offset losses of one member corporation against the income of other members of the group. It also permits the group to defer the reporting of a gain from an intercompany sale of property until the property is sold outside the group or the purchasing member claims tax depreciation deductions. Dividends received from members of the group are eliminated from the recipient's income.

Disadvantages of filing consolidated returns

The principal disadvantage of filing a consolidated return is having to comply with the very complex Treasury regulations which govern them. These regulations have the force of law and any affiliated group electing to file a consolidated return consents to be bound by them. Once elected, the consolidated return filing procedure may not be discontinued without IRS consent, which is difficult to obtain. Lesser disadvantages include the deferral of deductions for losses on intercompany transactions and the additional recordkeeping required. On balance, however, the advantages of a consolidated return usually outweigh the disadvantages.

Many states do not permit the filing of consolidated returns. Eligibility depends on the particular state in which a taxpayer does business. Some states, such as California, may require combined returns for unitary businesses in certain circumstances.

13. Taxation of foreign corporations

A foreign corporation is subject to U.S. income tax on income derived from business conducted in the U.S. and on passive income from U.S. sources. In many cases, the U.S. tax liability of the foreign corporation is governed by a tax treaty. In general, a treaty limits the taxation of U.S. industrial and commercial activities to the profits attributable to a permanent U.S. establishment. A tax treaty also may provide for withholding tax rates on passive income that are lower than the flat 30% U.S. statutory rate.

Trading as a branch

Subject to any applicable double taxation treaty, a foreign corporation trading in the U.S. as a branch is subject to U.S. income tax on the income effectively connected with the conduct of its trade or business within the U.S. This income includes profits from operations (trading), capital gains, interest, dividends, rents, and other income which arises from the U.S. business.

The tax liability of a foreign corporation on effectively connected income is determined in the same manner as that of a domestic corporation. Separate accounts must be maintained for the branch operation and elaborate rules are provided for determining whether interest, dividends, and other passive income are attributable to the branch.

Fixed or determinable annual or periodical income from U.S. sources (interest, dividends, rents, and the like) which is not effectively connected with the U.S. business is taxed at the flat 30% statutory or lower treaty rate. However, a foreign corporation or nonresident alien individual may elect to treat investment income from U.S. real estate as effectively connected to take advantage of deductions and lower tax rates.

In general, any income which is derived from assets used in the U.S. business is effectively connected income. Income also is effectively connected if the activities of the U.S. branch contributed materially to earning the income. Home office expenses, including interest, allocable to branch activities also are deductible.

Under the Foreign Investment in Real Property Tax Act (FIRPTA), gain from the disposition of a foreign-owned interest in U.S. real property is treated as effectively connected with a U.S. trade or business whether or not the owner has such a business.

Other capital gains are fully exempt from U.S. tax if they are neither:

- effectively connected with the conduct of a U.S. trade or business; nor

- fixed or determinable annual or periodical income from sources within the U.S.

A supplemental tax is imposed on U.S. branch profits of foreign corporations, unless the profits are reinvested in the U.S. The tax base generally is the branch's taxable income reduced by U.S. and foreign income taxes and the profits reinvested in the branch. This tax was enacted in 1986 effective for 1987 and later years. It does not apply if its application is inconsistent with tax treaties.

The rate of branch tax is the same as the statutory dividend withholding tax rate, currently 30%. If the foreign corporation is resident in a treaty country, the branch tax rate is reduced to the treaty rate applicable to direct-investment dividends. However, this relief is not available if the majority of the foreign corporation's beneficial individual owners are not residents of the treaty country.

The branch tax is intended to impose the same U.S. tax on a branch as that imposed on a U.S. subsidiary of a foreign corporation which repatriates profits.

Interest paid by the branch is treated as if paid by a U.S. corporation. Therefore, this interest is considered to have a U.S. source and is subject to the 30% statutory withholding tax. However, the tax may be reduced or eliminated by another provision of the Internal Revenue Code or a treaty. Treaty relief is not available if the majority of the foreign corporation's beneficial individual owners are not residents of the treaty country.

This treatment also applies to home office and other interest deductions allocated to the branch which exceed the branch's interest payments. (Interest allocations may occur if the branch's debt is disproportionately small compared to the foreign corporation's total debt.)

Income from U.S. subsidiaries

Profits

The profits of foreign-owned U.S. subsidiaries are taxable in the same manner as those of any other domestic corporation.

Dividends

A U.S. subsidiary must withhold a 30% income tax on dividends paid to its foreign parent unless a lower withholding rate applies under a tax treaty. Most treaties provide a lower rate, some as low as 5%.

No withholding is required if the dividends are effectively connected with the conduct of a U.S. trade or business by the foreign parent.

Interest

A U.S. corporation must withhold an income tax at the 30% statutory or lower treaty rate on interest paid to shareholders owning 10% or more of its stock. Several treaties reduce or eliminate this tax for interest paid to residents of the treaty country.

There is no withholding on interest effectively connected with the conduct of a U.S. trade or business by the recipient.

Royalties

A 30% income tax must be withheld from royalties for the use of U.S. patent rights and from U.S. source copyright royalties unless the payment is subject to a lower rate under a double taxation treaty.

Capital gains

If a foreign parent corporation realizes a capital gain on disposition of its investment in a U.S. subsidiary, no U.S. tax liability is incurred.

Service fees

Arm's-length payments for items such as management services, technical assistance, and use of know-how may be made by a U.S. subsidiary to its foreign parent. Such payments are tax-deductible business expenses if they benefit the U.S. subsidiary and are not primarily stewardship expenses of the parent. If these services are performed in the U.S., the income may be subject to the 30% statutory withholding tax unless a lower rate applies under a treaty.

14. Taxation of foreign operations

Taxation of foreign income

A U.S. domestic corporation which has foreign operations will be taxed as follows:

Branch income

The income of a foreign branch of a U.S. domestic corporation is subject to U.S. income tax for the tax year in which it is earned, whether or not it is repatriated. Income tax payments may be deferred if foreign income cannot be remitted to the U.S. because of foreign law or government action.

The foreign tax paid by the branch may be deducted or it may be claimed as a credit against the U.S. income tax liability attributable to the branch's income.

Income from foreign subsidiaries

The income of a foreign subsidiary generally is not subject to U.S. tax until it is repatriated through management fees, royalties, rents, interest, or dividends. However, a domestic corporation is subject to U.S. tax on its interest in certain income of a controlled foreign corporation (CFC). A CFC is a corporation incorporated outside the U.S. and controlled by U.S. shareholders. A foreign corporation is controlled by U.S. shareholders if more than 50% of its stock (by voting power or value) is owned on any day of the corporation's tax year by U.S. persons owning 10% or more of the corporation's voting power.

Income currently taxable to a 10% or more U.S. shareholder (known as 'Subpart F income') includes:

- income from insurance or reinsurance of U.S. risks;
- foreign personal holding company income (i.e. passive investment income);
- foreign base company sales income (income from sales to, or purchases from, a related person of property produced, and sold for use, outside the CFC's country of incorporation);

- foreign base company services income (income from services performed for a related person outside the CFC's country of incorporation);
- foreign base company shipping income;
- foreign base company oil-related income;
- bribe and boycott income;
- increase in earnings invested in U.S. property;
- net gains from the sale of property which does not generate active income;
- net gains from commodity transactions;
- net foreign currency gains from certain transactions in financial assets; and
- passive leasing income.

Foreign base company income and insurance income of a CFC are not taxable currently if in total they are less than the smaller of 5% of the corporation's gross income or $1,000,000.

All of a CFC's income is taxable currently to the U.S. shareholders if more than 70% of the corporation's gross income is base company and insurance income.

Capital gains

Gains on sales of shares in foreign subsidiaries or on disposals of foreign branch assets by a U.S. corporation are subject to U.S. income tax.

Dividends

Dividends from non-U.S. sources are subject to U.S. income tax for the tax year in which they are received. Distributions from previously taxed subpart F income are exempt from tax.

Interest income

Interest income from foreign operations is subject to U.S. income tax when accrued or received subject to relief for foreign withholding tax.

Royalties received

Foreign royalties are taxable when accrued or received, with credit for foreign withholding taxes.

15. Partnerships and joint ventures

Tax treatment

A partnership doing business in, or having income from sources within, the U.S. must file a return of income for its tax year, regardless of the amount of income or loss. The partnership is not a taxable entity and it files only an information return. Each partner reports his share of the partnership's income or loss on his own income tax return.

A partnership's business income is computed in substantially the same way as that of a corporation, except that it is not entitled to the special deduction for dividends received and may not gross-up foreign dividends for foreign taxes paid. The partners' shares of each of specified categories of income and deductions are disclosed separately on the return.

Generally, elections affecting the partnership's taxable income are made by the partnership. However, the election to credit or deduct foreign taxes is made by each partner.

A partner's share of the partnership's income, deductions, and credits generally is determined by the partnership agreement. However, the agreement will be ignored by the IRS if it lacks substantial economic effect.

Each partner must include all partnership items in his own return in the same amount and manner as reported by the partnership. If the partner wishes to report the item in a different way or amount, he must notify the IRS. If he fails to do so, the IRS can unilaterally recompute his tax to conform to the partnership's method of reporting.

Severe penalties are imposed if a partnership fails to file a return.

Taxation of foreign partners

A foreign corporation or nonresident alien who is a partner in a U.S. or foreign partnership is taxable on his share of the partnership's:

- income (including capital gains) effectively connected with the conduct of a U.S. trade or business; and
- U.S. source fixed or determinable annual or periodical income.

A noncorporate resident alien partner is taxed on his share of the partnership's worldwide income and capital gains.

Joint ventures

A joint venture is treated as a partnership for U.S. tax purposes.

Part Five

Taxes on Individuals and Other Taxes

16. Taxation of individuals

Territoriality and residence

All individual taxpayers fall into one of two categories:

- U.S. resident individuals, whether alien or citizen; or
- nonresident aliens.

Residents are subject to U.S. income tax on worldwide income and capital gains, although they are generally able to claim relief for foreign taxes. Nonresident aliens are subject to U.S. income tax only on:

- income from personal services rendered in the U.S.;
- income (including capital gains) effectively connected with the conduct of a U.S. trade or business; and
- U.S. source fixed or determinable annual or periodic income.

A U.S. gift tax is imposed on worldwide gifts of property by U.S. citizens or residents. In the case of nonresident donors, the tax is imposed only on gifts of real and tangible personal property situated in the U.S. The U.S. also imposes an estate tax at death on the worldwide property of a U.S. citizen or resident.

In the case of a nonresident alien, the estate tax applies only to property situated in the U.S. However, property such as life insurance proceeds, bank deposits, certain debt obligations, and works of art on loan for exhibition are exempt. Estate tax treaties modify these and other general rules.

An additional tax is imposed on specified generation-skipping transfers, either by gift or at death. Many states impose their own estate or inheritance taxes and a few states also impose gift taxes.

Residence

An alien is treated as a U.S. resident for a calendar year if he:

- has the right to reside permanently in the U.S. as an immigrant at any time during the calendar year (the "green card" test); or
- is present in the U.S. for a substantial period of time (the "substantial presence" test).

The substantial presence test is met if days present in the U.S. during the current year, plus one-third of the days present during the preceding year, plus one-sixth of the days present during the second preceding year equal or exceed 183 days (an average of 122 days each year). However, an alien present in the U.S. for less than 31 days in any tax year will not be classified as a resident for that year under this test.

Example:

Lionel Jones, a British national, was present in the U.S. during the following periods:

Year	Period in US	Number of days
1985	July 1 – Dec 31	184
1986	All year	365
1987	Jan 1 – Jan 31	31

Jones' residence test is calculated as follows:

Year	Multiplier		Days present		Total
1985	1/6	x	184	=	31
1986	1/3	x	365	=	122
1987	1	x	31	=	31
					184

Since the total days computed under this test exceed 182, Jones meets the substantial presence test for 1987, even though he left the country on January 31. However, if he had left on January 30, he would be a non-resident.

An alien meeting the substantial presence test nevertheless may be treated as a nonresident if he is present in the U.S. for less than 183 days during the tax year, establishes that his connections with a foreign country are closer than with the U.S., and that he has a "tax home" (generally the individual's principal place of business) in that country. An abode in the U.S. does not automatically exclude a foreign tax home.

Thus, in the above example, Jones is taxed as a resident alien for 1986, since he was present in the U.S. for 183 days or more. However, if he can establish his tax home in another country and demonstrate his closer connection with that country, he will be treated as a nonresident alien for 1987.

Any day on which an individual is unable to leave the U.S. because of a medical condition that arose while present in the U.S. is not treated as a U.S. day for the substantial presence test.

An alien classified as a U.S. resident for three consecutive years, who is a U.S. resident during one of the next three years, will be subject to U.S. tax as a resident for all intermediate years on his effectively connected U.S. business income and other U.S. source income.

An alien moving to the U.S. late in a year will fail to satisfy the substantial presence test for that year. Nevertheless, he may elect resident status for that year provided he meets this test for the following year. This election enables the alien to file a joint return with his spouse and obtain the benefit of personal exemptions and itemized deductions. To qualify for this election, the alien:

- may not be a U.S. resident for the year preceding the election year;
- must be present in the U.S. for at least 31 consecutive days in the election year; and
- must be present in the U.S. for at least 75% of the number of days in the period beginning with the first day of the 31-day U.S. presence test and ending with the last day of the election year. For this purpose, up to five days during which he was absent from the U.S. may be counted as U.S. days.

Income tax

U.S. residents, whether or not citizens, are subject to tax on their worldwide income, including compensation, capital gains, interest, dividends, rents, royalties, professional fees, pensions, annuities, and alimony.

The rates are graduated. Separate rate schedules are provided for single taxpayers, married couples filing joint returns, married couples filing separate returns, and unmarried heads of households. The 1988 schedules for single taxpayers and married couples filing joint returns are as follows:

	Rate
Single taxpayers:	
Taxable income up to $17,850	15%
Taxable Income over $17,850	28% of excess
Married couples:	
Taxable income up to $29,750	15%
Taxable income over $29,750	28% of excess

A 5% surcharge imposed to phase out the benefit of personal exemptions and the 15% rate raises the effective rate to 33% at certain income levels.

Remuneration

All remuneration, including most benefits and facilities derived from employment, is taxable. Fringe benefits are included in compensation at fair market value. These include living allowances, housing allowances, costs of educating children, and vacations. Tax exemption or deferral is available for some benefits, such as:

- qualified pension and profit-sharing plans;
- health and accident plans;
- reimbursed moving expenses;
- meals or lodging furnished for the employer's convenience.

Foreign personnel

Subject to applicable double taxation treaties, compensation received for services rendered in the U.S. is considered derived from U.S. sources unless:

- the services are performed by a nonresident alien temporarily present in the U.S. for not more than 90 days during the tax year;
- the compensation does not exceed $3,000; and
- the services are performed for:
  - a nonresident alien or foreign partnership or corporation not engaged in trade or business in the U.S.; or
  - a foreign business branch of a U.S. citizen or resident or a domestic partnership or corporation.

Foreign pensions

Foreign-source pensions received by persons resident in the U.S. are taxable. Pensions paid to nonresident aliens generally are taxable in the U.S. at the lower of 30% or the treaty rate if the services were performed in the U.S.

Business profits

The business profits of individuals carrying on a business or profession in the U.S. are taxed in a similar way to those of corporations. The same deductions generally are available.

Capital gains

Capital gains are taxed at the same rate as ordinary income for tax years beginning after 1987. Capital losses are deductible against capital gains and up to $3,000 of ordinary income. Unused capital losses are carried forward for the individual's lifetime. There are relief provisions for:

- sales or exchanges of principal residences;
- exchanges of stock or securities in connection with corporate reorganizations;
- exchanges of certain other investments or business property; and
- involuntary conversions of property.

Deductions

Business-related deductions

An individual may deduct any necessary traveling expenses (excluding traveling between home and work) and other ordinary and necessary expenses incurred in the performance of his duties. The individual also may deduct entertainment expenses subject to the rules previously discussed for corporations.

If an employer reimburses an employee for his expenses, the employer may deduct the reimbursement. In such case, the reimbursement is not taxable income to the employee provided he has properly accounted to the employer for the reimbursed expenses.

Dues and subscriptions to employment-related organizations and publications are deductible.

If the individual is self-employed, the business-related expenses are deductible in arriving at his gross income subject to tax. If he is an employee, these deductions are allowable only as miscellaneous itemized deductions. As a result, they are deductible only if:

- the employee does not claim the standard deduction; and
- to the extent they exceed 2% of adjusted gross income.

Moving expense reimbursements attributable to employment or self-employment are includible in gross income. If specified conditions are met, an itemized deduction may be allowable for a limited amount of moving expenses.

Net operating losses

Losses from business operations may be offset against income of any description (including capital gains) arising in the same tax year. A net operating loss in excess of current income is carried back three years and then forward 15 years. An individual may elect to waive the carryback of a loss and only carry it forward.

Non-business expenses

The following personal expenses are deductible as itemized deductions:

- state and local income taxes;
- real estate taxes;
- personal property taxes;
- charitable contributions to U.S. charities (subject to limitations based on adjusted gross income);
- mortgage interest attributable to a first and second residence;
- investment interest up to the amount of investment income;
- medical and dental expenses to the extent they exceed 7.5% of adjusted gross income; and
- casualty and theft losses to the extent they exceed $100 for each loss and 10% of adjusted gross income for all losses during the year.

Investment interest in excess of net investment income and personal (consumer) interest are not deductible at all after 1990. Limited amounts of these expenses are deductible in 1987, 1988, 1989 and 1990. Disallowed investment interest may be carried over and deducted in future years against investment income.

Standard deduction

A standard deduction may be claimed if it is greater than the taxpayer's itemized deductions.

Personal exemptions

Individual taxpayers are entitled to personal exemptions for themselves and their dependents. These exemptions benefit only low-income taxpayers.

Credits

An individual is entitled to a credit for foreign taxes paid on foreign income which is subject to U.S. tax. The credit is limited to the same proportion of the U.S. tax as the foreign-source income is of total income. An individual is also entitled to the research and targeted jobs credits.

Alternative minimum tax

Individuals are subject to an alternative minimum tax (AMT) of 21% which is applied to the AMT base. The AMT is paid only to the extent it exceeds the income tax.

The AMT base is taxable income plus tax preferences, less an exemption of $40,000 for married couples filing a joint return or $30,000 for an unmarried individual. This exemption is phased out for higher-income individuals. The phase-out is equal to 25c for each $1 of AMT taxable income exceeding $150,000 for joint return filers or $112,500 for unmarried individuals. The exemption is completely phased out when AMT taxable income reaches $310,000 for joint return filers or $232,500 for unmarried individuals.

The more common preferences for individuals are:

- excess depreciation;

- tax-exempt interest on specified private activity bonds;

- charitable contributions of appreciated property;

- deferred income from certain installment sales;

- percentage depletion;

- intangible drilling costs;

- incentive stock options;

- passive losses;

- state and local taxes;

- interest expense;

- medical expense; and

- miscellaneous itemized deductions.

The rules previously discussed for corporations regarding net operating losses and tax credits also apply to individuals except that no investment credit is allowable.

Joint income tax returns

Married couples may file joint income tax returns which usually are more advantageous than separate returns. The rate schedule for a joint income tax return subjects a substantially higher amount of income to the lowest tax rate.

A joint return may not be filed if either spouse is a nonresident alien. However, a married couple comprising a U.S. citizen or resident and a nonresident alien may elect to file a joint return if they agree to be taxed on their worldwide income. A similar election is available if the non-resident alien becomes a U.S. resident during a tax year.

Unified taxes on transfers of property

There is no wealth tax in the U.S.

The federal gift, estate, and generation skipping transfer taxes comprise an integrated system for taxing gratuitous transfers of property. The gift tax is imposed on transfers during life and the estate tax applies to transfers at death. The generation skipping transfer tax is an additional tax which is imposed on transfers that skip one or more generations. This tax captures the additional gift or estate tax that would have been paid if the property had been transferred from one generation to the next without skipping.

Example:

A family consists of a grandfather (A), his son (B), and his grandson (C). There is no generation skipping transfer if A gives B $5,000,000. On the other hand, there is a generation skipping transfer if A gives $5,000,000 to C while B is alive, since this transfer avoids the tax that would have been incurred if A had given $5,000,000 to B, and B had given it to C.

The top gift, estate, and generation skipping transfer tax rates are 55% through 1992 and 50% thereafter. Proper planning for effective use of various exclusions and exemptions can minimize or eliminate these taxes.

Taxable gifts

U.S. citizens and residents

Gifts are valued at fair market value on the date of the gift. Married couples may consent to treat all gifts made by them to third parties during a calendar year as made one-half by each spouse. This treatment is called "gift-splitting".

Each donor (including a spouse who consents to gift-splitting) may exclude up to $10,000 of gifts to each donee during any calendar year. This exclusion does not apply to gifts of future interests, which are interests in property that are to commence in use, possession, or enjoyment at some future date. However, the exclusion is available for gifts of future interests that benefit a donee under age 21 if certain conditions are met.

Most gifts to spouses are not taxable. This is accomplished by allowance of a marital deduction from total reported gifts. There also is a deduction for charitable gifts.

Nonresident aliens

Nonresident aliens are subject to gift tax on transfers of property located in the U.S., such as real estate, business assets, and stock in U.S. corporations. Gift-splitting is not available if either spouse is a non-resident alien. The marital deduction generally is not allowable if the donor is a nonresident alien. Charitable deductions are available only for gifts to domestic charities.

The U.S. has gift tax treaties with several foreign countries to avoid double taxation of gifts. Some of these treaties permit gift-splitting and a partial or full marital deduction.

Computation of taxable estate

U.S. citizens and residents

Property in a decedent's estate is valued at fair market value at the date of death to determine the gross estate. However, the executor may elect to value the property at its fair market value six months after death if this election reduces the gross estate and the estate tax.

The following deductions are allowable in arriving at the taxable estate:

- funeral expenses;

- mortgages, liens, and other debts of the decedent;

- bequests and other transfers to the surviving spouse;

- charitable bequests.

Administration expenses and net losses during administration may be claimed either as an estate tax deduction or as an income tax deduction.

Nonresident aliens

Any property owned at death by a nonresident alien which is situated in the U.S. is taxable. It is valued under the rules applicable to U.S. citizens or residents. Only a proportionate amount of otherwise deductible expenses, debts, and losses may be claimed as deductions from the gross estate. This proportion is determined by the following fraction:

$$\frac{\text{Value of gross estate situated in the U.S.}}{\text{Value of entire gross estate (wherever situated)}}$$

No deductions are allowed unless the estate tax return discloses the value of the gross estate situated outside the U.S.

The marital deduction generally is not available.

Computation of gift and estate tax

U.S. citizens and residents

The gift and estate taxes are imposed under a unified transfer tax system. There are 16 tax brackets, ranging from 18% to 50%, with a 17th bracket at 55% applicable through 1992. Gifts are reported annually but the tax rate is determined by the taxpayer's cumulative lifetime gifts. Each taxpayer is entitled to a tax credit of $192,800 which is applied first to lifetime gifts and then to transfers at death. This credit permits $600,000 to be transferred tax-free. An additional 5% tax is imposed on very large estates. The estate tax base is computed by adding taxable gifts made after 1976 to the taxable estate. The gifts are valued at their date of gift fair market value. A gross estate tax is computed on this base. The following credits are allowable in determining the net estate tax:

- gift taxes paid on post-1976 gifts;

- the $192,800 unified credit;

- state death taxes; and

- foreign death taxes.

There also is a limited credit for estate tax paid on the transfer of property to the decedent by a transferor who died within ten years before, or within two years after, the decedent's death.

Nonresident aliens

The computation of the gift tax is the same as for U.S. residents except that no unified credit is available for nonresident donors.

In computing the estate tax, the following credits may be claimed:

- gift tax on gifts added to the taxable estate;

- a $3,600 unified credit (the equivalent of a $60,000 exemption); and

- a limited amount of state death taxes.

The estate of a nonresident alien is subject to estate tax rates ranging from 6% to 30% and is reduced by a credit of $3,600.

The limited credit for estate tax on prior transfers also may be allowable. There is no credit for foreign death taxes.

The U.S. has concluded death tax treaties with several foreign countries to avoid double taxation. Under some of these treaties, a partial or full marital deduction may be allowed.

State gift, estate, and inheritance taxes

U.S. citizens and residents, as well as nonresident aliens, may be subject to state transfer taxes. The rate and method of computation are different for each state.

Social security

Social security system

The U.S. operates a social security system which provides benefits as follows:

- old age, survivors, and disability insurance;
- limited hospital and supplementary medical insurance for individuals age 65 and over; and
- unemployment insurance.

Employer contributions

All business employers are required to contribute to the Social Security System to fund retirement and health benefits. Employers also pay a federal unemployment tax which supplements the unemployment benefit systems of the various states. Contributions are based on a percentage of employees' remuneration up to a maximum per employee which is adjusted annually. Generally, foreign employers of nonresident aliens performing services in the U.S. also must make these contributions.

Employee contributions

Employees also must pay contributions to the U.S. Social Security System. The employee's contribution is the same percentage of the employee's earnings, up to the specified limit, as paid by the employer. Employees do not contribute to the unemployment insurance fund.

Generally, nonresident aliens employed in the U.S. must contribute to the social security system in the same way as U.S. citizens or residents. The U.S. has social security agreements with several foreign countries which eliminate dual coverage and contributions for the same work.

Contributions by self-employed persons

The self-employed pay social security contributions for retirement and health benefits, based on a fixed percentage of their self-employment income, up to a maximum amount. The self-employed do not pay unemployment taxes.

Benefits

Foreign workers employed in the U.S. may receive social security benefits in the same manner as U.S. workers once a satisfactory U.S. contributions history has been established. Certain social security agreements with other countries provide benefits without the need for a U.S. contributions history. Benefits are paid only for retirement, disability, or death.

17. Other taxes

Federal taxes

Excise taxes

Federal excise taxes are imposed on a variety of U.S. produced goods and services, including:

- foreign insurance and reinsurance policies;
- alcohol;
- tobacco;
- air transportation;
- telephone and teletypewriter services;
- gasoline and petroleum;
- tires;
- heavy trucks and trailers;
- non-commercial aviation fuel;
- diesel fuel (unless used on a farm for farming purposes);
- coal;
- gas-guzzling automobiles;
- hazardous waste; and
- firearms.

Customs duties

Customs duties are imposed on imported goods at varying rates subject to many exemptions.

The U.S. income tax basis of property imported into the U.S. from a related party cannot exceed the value claimed for customs purposes.

State and local taxes

Various taxes are imposed by the District of Columbia, the 50 states, and their respective counties, cities, and other local jurisdictions. The Commonwealth of Puerto Rico and U.S. possessions also impose taxes.

The major taxes imposed by the states are corporate income taxes (including franchise taxes based on income), individual income taxes, and sales and use taxes.

Real estate taxes

Real estate taxes are assessed and collected by city, county, or other local authorities. These taxes provide funds for public services, including education, fire and police services, roads, sanitation, and street lighting. They are assessed on property owners at varying levels according to appraised values. Agricultural property may be taxed at lower rates.

Stamp taxes

Many types of commercial and legal documents must be stamped to denote the payment of taxes. The rate may be fixed or *ad valorem*. Stamp taxes are payable on the legal conveyance of property but not on the transfer of beneficial ownership. In general, documents need not be stamped unless they are executed in the U.S. or they relate to property situated in, or to transactions carried out in, the U.S. The effect of failure to stamp a document is that the document may not be legally admissible in evidence. Penalties may be payable for late stamping.

Additional taxes

Other state and local taxes include:

- franchise taxes on corporate capital stock and surplus;
- gift, estate, and inheritance taxes;
- personal property taxes;
- severance taxes on oil and gas; and
- motor vehicle and driver licenses.

BDO offices

BDO has offices in the following countries:

Argentina	Luxembourg
Australia	Macau
Austria	Malaysia
Belgium	Mexico
Bolivia	Monaco
Brazil	Namibia
Brunei	Netherlands
Canada	Netherlands Antilles
Chile	New Zealand
Colombia	Nigeria
Costa Rica	Norway
Cyprus	Oman
Denmark	Pakistan
Egypt	Peru
Finland	Portugal
France	Saudi Arabia
Germany	Seychelles
Guernsey	Singapore
Hong Kong	South Africa
India	Spain
Ireland	Sweden
Isle of Man	Switzerland
Italy	Taiwan
Japan	United Arab Emirates
Jersey	United Kingdom
Kenya	United States of America
Korea	Uruguay
Kuwait	Venezuela
Lebanon	

The address of the International Secretariat of BDO is:

World Trade Center Amsterdam
Tower A
Floor 11
Strawinskylaan 1109
1007 XX Amsterdam
Netherlands   International Secretary: Paul van Elten